The Power of the Plan

Empowering the Leader in You

by Douglas Land and David Barrett

First Edition

Oshawa, Ontario

The Power of the Plan:
Empowering the Leader in You
by Douglas Land and David Barrett

Managing Editor:	Kevin Aguanno
Editor:	Susan Andres
Typesetting:	Carolyn Prior
Cover Design:	?????
eBook Conversion:	Carolyn Prior

Published by:
Multi-Media Publications Inc.
1050 Simcoe St. North, Suite 110
Oshawa, ON, Canada, L1G 4W5
http://www.mmpubs.com/

Paperback	ISBN-13:	9781554891368
eBook	ISBN-13:	9781554891375

Published in Canada. Printed simultaneously in Canada, the United States of America, Australia, and the United Kingdom.

CIP data available from the publisher.

Dedication

This book is dedicated to our wives, whose biggest and most challenging project has been to keep us sane and to our most amazing children, their partners and Doug's granddaughter. Thank you for just being you.

Douglas Land and David Barrett

Table of Contents

Acknowledgement

We would like to acknowledge the input and encouragement, whether consciously or not, of all the literally thousands of people from all walks of life who have sat in our classes, workshops or conferences. Truly, we have learned as much or more from them than they have from us.

We also want to acknowledge our colleagues in the project management community who have never failed to be an encouragement and guide to our careers in this field.

Finally and most importantly, we want to acknowledge the tremendous influence on our lives and careers of Dr. Goldwyn, (Bud), Lush, MSc, PhD, FRCPM; Chairman & Chief Technical Officer, Atocrates Project Sciences. A mentor and a friend and we are deeply grateful to him and his wife Tena.

Douglas Land & David Barrett

The Power of The Plan

Introduction

In 2007, Bob and Linda decided to renovate their house. They wanted to open the old kitchen and dining room into one big family area, build a new kitchen, and build a new patio in the back. Money was a little tight, so they decided to forgo a general contractor and do it themselves. After all, it looked easy on TV. An architect was out of the question, as he or she would cost too much money, so they asked a friend just out of design school to pull together the drawings. Then, they handed the drawings to a professional to obtain the necessary permits. That's when the fun began.

Very quickly, our friends discovered that managing a home renovation was not as easy as it looked on TV. They believed that it was about simply developing and managing a good schedule. They soon learned that it had as much to do with managing the budget and knowing how to control the typical cost overruns, managing all the changes typical in such an initiative, and managing all the people such as the contractors, the inspectors, the neighbors, and even the kids. Most important, it had to do with understanding what they wanted in the first place.

This book was written for Bob and Linda. It is also for Joan on the local school board, who has been asked to lead the team responsible for the Fall Fun Fair, the major fund raising event of the year, but is not sure she has the experience to do so. This book is for Sally who has been asked to spearhead a new e-marketing campaign at her company. This book is for Jim, who will manage the new office relocation from Halifax to Vancouver. It is for George and Barb, who want to go on a one-year trip around the world. In short, this book is for anyone facing a decision to lead a project or initiative, or to take advantage of an opportunity, however small or large.

This book will empower the leader in you. Managing any sized project or initiative involving others immediately puts you in a leadership role. The contractors, the suppliers, fellow employees, the volunteers, and even your family will look to you to lead them to the outcome. They want the leader in you to shine. They want the project to succeed as much as you do.

However, the leadership role can be unnerving, and fear—fear of commitment, fear of change, and fear of disrupted lives—holds many of us back from becoming the leaders we have dreamed of being. Some or all these fears might be legitimate; however, most of us can look back on missed opportunities and know in our heart of hearts that we failed to take advantage of them because we feared failing.

If you want to conquer your fears, to take the leap, to commit to the event, take on the renovation, or be the lead on the office move, then read on. This book will help you decide to say yes. Our premise is simple—having a good plan will remove the fear factor and empower you to be the leader you want to be. The Power of the Plan will enable you to accomplish your goals and dreams.

We use the analogy of a door placed in front of you. Beyond the door lies the project or opportunity you are thinking about leading or taking. Once you open the door and walk through, you are committed; there is no turning back. However, before you decide to open the door, you must spend some time analyzing the decision. Should you take this on? Should you say yes? What will it cost in time and commitment?

Once you decide to say yes, we are here to guide you through the next steps to plan, execute, and close your project successfully. We will also show you how to monitor and control your project while you execute it. We want to give you simple and understandable steps to success.

About planning, someone once commented that managing any initiative involving a group of people, a budget, and a time line was a snap—just buy the latest project management scheduling tool, and it will take care of it for you. Someone else added, "Heck, who needs a complicated scheduling tool—just use a spreadsheet."

Well, we wish this were true, but it isn't. We like the analogy of a word processor—this wonderful tool does not create great writers, nor does a simple-to-use desktop publishing tool make great, or even good, graphic artists. You know the saying, garbage in—garbage out. A good plan comes from sound, intuitive, analytical, and creative thinking, not software. A good plan comes from you, your contacts, your research, and your best judgment. The root of successful projects lies in the planning stages. Once you formulate a "big picture" plan that focuses on your vision of the product, the time, money, and people aspects of managing a project, you need to create the detailed plan.

You first visualize the project and the plan from an altitude of about 15,000 feet. Then, you want to come right down to the treetops, look at the project again, and develop a detailed plan to guide you through the project.

The Plan consists of six elements:

1. The Charter: the "big picture" or the scope statement.

2. The Work Breakdown: what needs to be done

3. The People: the human resources who will do the work

4. The Time: estimating how long will the project take and when each element happens

5. The Budget: the detailed costs

6. The Risks: how you manage the risks involved from start to finish

Plans vary in size, detail, and level of complexity, but the fundamental elements are always the same. Understand that the word scale is important. It takes about five minutes to create a plan that uses some of these elements for a simple project to paint a room in your home, while creating a plan for a major fundraising gala for your local hospital involves all these elements and takes much longer. In this book, we look at each of these elements in detail, using project examples of renovating a kitchen and holding a fundraising gala.

Step 1 deals with that door in front of you. Once you commit, we show you how to develop a strong plan that will enable you to deal with managing the work, developing and controlling a budget, choosing and developing a great team of employees or volunteers, communicating effectively, and successfully closing your project.

We, the authors, come from the world of professional project management. We are here to take what we have learned from that world and help you apply that knowledge to your daily initiatives, whatever the size and application. We will spend the next pages and a few visits to our website empowering you to be a great leader by presenting you with easy-to-understand tools and techniques that anyone can use. Using our book involves the Internet. We want to help you navigate these pages, and we want to help you with an electronic version of all the tools about which we talk. We provide you our website, so you can pick a tool, document, or template about which we have talked.

Let's get started!

Remember, as we go through the book we will refer back to our web site: www.ThePowerofThePlan.com

The Power of The Plan

CHAPTER 1

Should You Open the Door?

In 2006, a group of well-meaning people decided to create a huge event to raise money for the Cancer Society. This core group spread the word among friends and family, and the buzz quickly began. It was the talk of the town or, at least, of their neighborhood. The idea was to rent a high-end hall, seek major corporate sponsors, hire a very popular band, and sell tickets at $100 a head.

It was easy to create a budget. The group decided on $2,500 for the space, $1,500 for the band, and $50 a head for food. Money would come in from 500 people at $100 each and 10 corporate sponsors at $2,500 each. As you can see, it looked as if they could write a very generous check, maybe for as much as $45,000. Easy money!

The organizers were all Type A's and in this case each thought that he or she led the project. As a result, the organizers were uncoordinated from the start. One offered to book the band, but did not worry too much about the budget. The final cost would be $2,500, instead of $1,500. The one who called the hall to book the space forgot to read the fine print. There would be taxes on the space and food as well as tips for the service. Finally, the one responsible for finalizing the event's date booked it in late June, which was the same weekend as the Grand Prix race in the city.

Obviously, the event "tanked." When we say it tanked, we don't mean that it lost money. It made money—$1,800... but after months of selling, advertising, organizing and worrying, they broke even.

Then, why did it tank? Well, they didn't do their homework up front. They didn't stop amid all the initial enthusiasm to ask themselves whether they had the right pieces in place and the right assumptions in place to make this a successful event. They didn't pause before "Opening the Door" to be sure this was the right door to go through or that they wanted to go through the door this way.

In the final analysis, too many "leaders" made too many decisions on their own. Unrealistic assumptions informed a very poor initial budget. The marketing plan overestimated the response, partly because of the poor scheduling. Potential patrons could not attend both the fundraiser and the race. Furthermore, the city's hotels were full, and out-of-towners could not book accommodations.

So, you have an idea for an event, a product launch, or a marketing campaign, or someone has asked you to lead a project, and you must decide—can you do it? To make the right decision to go, or not to go, you must do some analysis. You must begin by asking yourself four key questions:

1. Do I have a clear vision of what I am trying to do?

2. Do I have enough time?

3. Do I have enough money?

4. Do I have the right people?

Not all these questions might apply to you, but you must spend the time addressing these questions, whatever your project is. You must be diligent—draw sketches, visit kitchen specialty shops if it's a new kitchen, talk to others who have successfully pulled off similar projects.

Learn to ask the difficult questions of others who have gone before you:

- How realistic was your budget estimate and time estimate?

- What are some less obvious tasks that can easily be overlooked when planning resources and schedules?

- How do you find the necessary volunteers?

- What went wrong? What would you do differently next time?

- Are there any special considerations?

Asking these questions is preliminary planning. The details will come later, but now is when you decide whether you will commit. The door is closed now, and you might feel anxious about opening it, but this early, high-level planning around these key questions will give you the confidence you need to open the door.

Have I a clear vision of what I am trying to do?

We suggested that one or more of these questions might not apply to you, but not this one. You must not avoid this question, as it is the most important. Without a clear vision of what you want to accomplish, dealing with the other questions is almost impossible. Take the time to dig into this question. Once you walk through that door, you will deal with details, people, and budgets. Before you get there, you had better know exactly what you want to accomplish. Do you have a clear vision of what the new kitchen should look like? Do you have a good idea of what the gala event should accomplish? These are all very important questions.

Look ahead and create a picture in your mind or on paper of what the product should look like. The project will rest on your shoulders, so you want to be in control. The plan's purpose is to give you better control, but you must know precisely what the goal or objective is. Before you can decide how much time, money, or help you will need, you must know as clearly and as precisely as possible what the result will be.

*Everyone involved along the way **wants** you to have this clear vision.*

They do not want a leader who waffles along the way—who changes his or her mind repeatedly. One element that contributes greatly to successful projects or events is momentum. If that momentum is repeatedly broken because you, the leader, are unsure or unclear of what the goal and interim objectives are, then it will be difficult to keep people around you interested. Everyone wants to work for someone who has the "vision" and knows exactly how to get there.

Caution: *Your vision can change.*

Your plan to accomplish that vision might change. Everyone understands that, but managing change successfully is a special talent. If you want to run an event, you will need to understand the key ideas of change management. We will deal with this special concept later in the book.

Consider the following when you formulate the big picture in your mind:

- Do you know why you are doing this project?
- What are your motives?
- What do you hope to get out of this?
- What do you hope to accomplish and why?

Later in the book, we talk about the team you will put together and the role passion plays in the successful contributions of volunteers. You must be passionate about this project also. If you take this project's leadership out of a sense of obligation or guilt, it will make your job much more difficult. If you are passionate and excited about doing it, the people around you will be passionate and excited too.

Have I enough time to make this happen?

 So many people out there will tell you, "Oh, it's a snap," or "plenty of time—no worries." But they are not being asked to lead the charge. You must look seriously at what you want to do and how much time it will take.

 You are not dealing with a detailed plan yet; you are just making estimates.

But you should look hard enough to be confident that you are not walking into a hornet's nest. Lack of time for enough planning is a serious stressor. Be realistic with yourself and others in this regard, because this factor, almost exclusively, causes projects to falter and fail.

 Tips:

It will always take more time than you think it will; remember Murphy's Law. Doubling your first estimate would not be too far off.

If you count on many deliverables, or handoffs, from others outside your control, realize that probably half these will be late.

If contracts are required for facilities, food, or other services, these will always take more time than you imagined to be signed off. Give people, including the retailers and vendors you use, lots of time to do their part.

Have I enough money to pull this off?

This is a difficult question to answer at this stage, but you must put some thought into it now. How much will this cost, and from where will this money come? Look at any quote for materials, labor, or other potentially variable costs with a very discriminating eye. For example, your project could cost at least 25% more, particularly if you are doing a renovation, because no one knows what they will find behind that wall or under that flooring. These projects are notorious for taking longer than estimated or using more material than estimated. You will find that it is easy to get to a 25% overrun.

Another potential area of cost overruns is because of overspending on appliances or materials. It is so easy to say yes to that slightly more expensive sink or mirror. It is a snap to go with the larger dishwasher, and it is easy to be talked into the nicer fabrics. Be wise about your purchases.

If you are looking at an event or project that relies on ticket sales to pay the costs, be very careful in estimating the number of buyers. An old established event is the easiest to manage, but a new event can be unpredictable.

 Tip: *Ask everyone around you to estimate the ticket sales. Take the average of the answers and then cut it by 25%. Now, relook at the budget. How does it look at this stage? We call this the "Worst Case Scenario," and now, you know what it is and how it will all work out if this is the result.*

If people or organizations promise you funds to make the event happen, ask yourself, "How sure is that money?" "What are the chances that those funds will not appear or not appear in the quantity promised?" A bit of risk management here is important. If the money doesn't pan out or you spend more than you make, someone's head (or reputation) will roll, and it might be yours!

Have I the right people for the project?

Many people will tell you that they can help, but note that they are not stepping up to take the lead on it. Again, discriminate in your estimates. Take the offers to help and cut them down by maybe a quarter. If you have twenty people offering to help you run the auction, count on fifteen. Understand the risk that they won't show. When we get to this issue in detail later, we will talk about a backup team and job shadowing.

Think about the component of key people for what you are trying to accomplish. Do you have them? Are these the right people? We will get into the people management side of all this later in the book, but at this stage, you want to be sure that you have the right people in key positions.

 You need two types of people: managers and workers, and they are equally important to you.

The managers lead a section of the project and report to you. They have a team of worker bees working for them. The workers—the builders, coders, painters, artists, salespeople, and others—are the engine.

Projects of any size are easy, until you start dealing with people. The challenges are many:

- Not having enough or having too many people

- Knowing each person's skills and talents

- Knowing how reliable your people are

- Toughest of all to manage—the intricacies of all those personalities.

 Caution: *Be very careful when dealing with family and close friends.*

When projects mess up, as they sometimes do, nerves are frayed, and eventually, fingers start pointing. When this happens, nobody wins. Do not let your best intentions and generosity ruin a good relationship.

Wrap-up

We have gone through the key questions or considerations as you look at the door, considering whether you should open it and step through. Now, you can make the Go/No Go decision. Will you take it on, agree to organize it, build it, develop it, or create it? Having diligently considered these project elements, you now have the confidence and the information to make a good decision. If you are satisfied and comfortable with the decision to go ahead, it is time to open that door and walk through it. We wish you much success and satisfaction!

Review Points:

- Is this the right door to go through?
- Is this the right way to go through the door?
- Have you talked with others who have successfully completed similar projects?
- Do you have a clear vision of what you are trying to do?
  - ° Can you create and maintain momentum?
  - ° What motivates you to do this project?
- Do you have enough time?
  - ° Remember Murphy's Law, and double your first estimate.
- Do you have enough money?
  - ° Anticipate at least a 25% overrun?
- Do you have the right people?
  - ° Anticipate 25% fewer volunteers than originally respond.
  - ° Who are your key people in key positions?
  - ° Do you have enough workers and managers?

CHAPTER 2

The Big Picture

The team at the office was asked to build a new website. The senior manager gave the team members the details, or so they thought, and off they went. They thought it would take about two weeks of work on top of the other work they had to do already. At first glance, it seemed like an easy job.

Move forward three weeks in time. Reality began to set in. The first problem was that building the website took much more work than they had anticipated. Then, they discovered that their senior manager had not communicated this project to any other manager in the company. It became apparent that not all the crucial personnel had been consulted. It seemed as though new functionality was coming out of the woodwork by the hour. Many were questioning current features. They began to hear the dreaded words: "Why are we even doing this, anyway?" The project was canceled in Week 4.

How often have you had someone approach you to help with a project? Maybe it sounded simple—sell a few tickets, help set up a hall or auditorium, attend a few meetings. However, when you started, you discovered that there was much more work involved than you were told. What's worse, the person who asked you to help had no idea of the magnitude of work required or any idea how to get it done.

Understanding the Big Picture is a key component to project success. In most circles this document is called the Project Charter. The charter is a simple, brief, readable document that defines the project's keys. You don't need it to be very detailed, but it should be detailed enough for anyone who will get involved to understand the vision and the major parameters around the initiative.

Do yourself and everyone involved in your project a huge favor—draw up a charter. Involve as many key leaders as possible in a brainstorming meeting. This is one time you'll find that the more heads you have around the table, the better off you will be.

 Caution: *Involve only the people leading the various project elements.*

This is not a time to seek the consensus of all the volunteers or all the Understanding the Big Picture is a key component to project success. In most circles this document is called the Project Charter. The Charter should be no longer than one page, and it should create an accurate a high-level "snapshot" of the overall project.

The advantages of using this tool are many:

- It forces you and your key leaders to think through and visualize the product, whether it's a kitchen or a fundraising event.

- It is an effective recruiting tool when you approach other volunteers to help. You can describe exactly

    ° What you want to accomplish?

    ° How long it will take?

    ° The commitment level of all the volunteers in time and workload.

- ° When, where, and how it will occur.

- ° By using this tool, your team will have a clear understanding of the expectations before they jump on board.

Tip: *Respect your coworkers' and volunteers' time. It pays big dividends when you are asked to lead the next project!*

We thought about these elements back on the other side of the door. Do you remember those crucial questions we asked you to consider about your vision and motivation, time, money, and resources? Now, it is time to put the answers to those questions on paper with the help of as many of your key people as you can gather. This is a bit of a brainstorming session that will shape those somewhat fuzzy ideas and plans.

The Charter should answer several key questions:

1. What is the project?

2. Who is it for?

3. How long will it take?

4. How much will it cost?

5. Who will be involved in the planning and execution of the project?

This is still a high-level overview of the plan. You don't have all the details or all the answers, but you are beginning to develop a good roadmap that will guide you and your team throughout the project. So you will want to keep it close at hand.

You might have to go back and update the charter. Note that I say, "might have to." Unfortunately, most often, managers forget to update the charter because they are so busy moving forward with the details. This crucial mistake can allow the project to take on a life of its own and result in confusion, delays, and frustration for everyone.

When things begin to feel as though they are getting out of control, and you are unsure of the direction in which you should move, your charter acts as a rudder on a ship and can steer the project back on course.

 If the project fundamentals change in any way, in scope or products, you must update the charter to reflect those changes.

Sometimes, it will be necessary to remind the team of the original intent and the reasons you are doing this in the first place. As we mentioned, your people will appreciate a good charter because it clearly defines the project, at least at a high level. Check out the website at www. thepoweroftheplan.com to see some samples of a Project Charter. In the meantime, here are a couple of examples:

Let's start with two examples of charters.

 The Kitchen Renovation

1. What is the project?

- You are going to renovate the kitchen in your home. You want the following from the renovation:

    ° A walkout to the back deck

- ° A new window looking east
- ° New counters and cupboards
- ° A cooking island
- ° New appliances
- ° An open concept to allow in-kitchen gathering
- ° Open to the living area

2. Who is it for?

- You want to think about how it is used—not just for the family's weekday meals, but also for hosting Saturday night dinner parties for friends or after-school or weekend gatherings for your kids' friends.

3. How long will it take?

- You want the kitchen completed by September 1. The kids are away most of the summer, and you can eat and cook out on the deck most of that time. You do not want to deal with the renovation in the fall. So, at this stage, you budget three months. As you detail the plan and see it could take longer, you will need to back up the start date to accommodate a completion by September 1.

4. How much will it cost?

- Only you can decide the overall budget. Our caution to you is to take the time to make sure you are estimating accurately. Do your homework!

5. Who will be involved?

- You want to design the renovations, having spent considerable time discussing it with friends and family and looking at other kitchens and design magazines. You are even prepared to do some finishing work; however, you have agreed that an outside contractor will do the major demolition and construction work.

 ## The Fundraising Gala

1. **What is the project?**

   - Charity gala. You have been asked to spearhead a fundraising event for a charitable organization involving youth in your city and about which you are deeply passionate. You have decided to have a somewhat formal, fully catered and served dinner, with service and entertainment provided by the young people benefiting from the fundraiser. Dinner and entertainment will be free; however, there will be a presentation and request for short-term and long-term financial support from those attending. You have set a target of 150–200 guests. Your goal is to raise between $10,000 and $15,000 in both short-term and long-term commitments.

2. **Who is it for?**

   - It will be for the people already supportive of the cause, but it will also target potential corporate and new personal donors. It will be by invitation only but will be well advertised and vigorously marketed by the recipients of the funds.

3. **How long will it take?**

   - Four months to plan and organize . You have decided that you want to hold it on a Thursday evening in the spring and have fixed a date of May 19. It is now early January, so you have nearly four months to plan and organize the event.

4. **How much will it cost?**

   - $1,500–$2,000. You know that you can get the
     facility donated with the kitchen, dinnerware,
     tablecloths, and so on. Volunteers will do the
     cooking and preparation, and all entertainment
     will be provided free. Your only costs are the
     food and drinks. You have allotted a per meal
     price of $10. Therefore, your preliminary budget
     is $1,500 to $2,000. This money will initially
     come out of your operating budget, but it will
     be reimbursed off the top from any one-time
     donation you receive at the event.

5. **Who will be involved?**

   - The Executive Committee with volunteers. The
     Executive Committee, which exists, will plan
     and coordinate the event. The members will
     structure a plan designating the key areas of
     responsibility. However, youth volunteers and
     willing parents and friends will do all work
     involved. There will be no need for any outside
     or paid help.

In both these examples of charters, we have formulated a
basic, high-level plan that will steer the project through
the next steps of detailed planning. The details involve
elements such as precise schedules, budgets, human
resources, and risks to the project. But the charter, as
outlined above, is your master plan, and should both anchor
and guide you and your team through the exciting times
ahead.

Can you see the value of a charter? Let's go back to what
we said at the beginning of this chapter—how often have
you wished the project leader you were asked to help would
have taken the time to develop this powerful planning tool?
We hope that you can see the benefits in helping you recruit
your team, guide your detailed planning, and hold the
project on course so you finish well.

Review Points:

- Have you created a charter, no longer than one page, creating an accurate picture of the overall project:

- What is the project?

- Whom is it for?

- How long will it take?

- How much will it cost?

- Who will be involved in the planning and execution of the project?

CHAPTER 3

Breaking Down the Work

Now that you have the charter or the big picture in place, it is time to drill down and collect details on your plan's various parts. Remember that we first looked at this project from an altitude of about 15,000 feet. The Charter was a closer look from an altitude of 10,000 feet. Now, we want to look at it from the treetops.

The first thing we must do is curb our enthusiasm and realistically define what work must be done and, just as important, what must not be done. This is often called a scope statement, and it involves listing what is "in scope" and what is "out of scope." In other words, you want to list clearly what work will be done (in scope), and what work will not be done (out of scope). It is all about clarity! The scope statement also tries to describe in detail what the end 'product' will look like. This exercise alone will help bring much clarity to your vision and will communicate your project boundaries to all involved.

By clearly describing the work to be done, you will more easily create a budget, figure out how long it will take, and decide who will complete the work.

If you are looking at managing a fundraising event, you would go through all the options, preferably with your organizing committee, to be sure that you agree on the different pieces of the puzzle. Some of them might be:

- Invitations: by word of mouth, e-mail, or mail?
- Dinner: yes or no; if yes, plated or buffet?
- Silent auction: yes or no?
- Cocktails: open or cash bar?
- Timing: start and end?

In the example of the kitchen renovation, which might seem a little more cut and dried, this step is equally important. You know what you are doing because of your charter. You are tearing out a wall between the kitchen and dining room and building a new kitchen. Moving to this next level, you might ask:

- Will you buy new appliances or reuse what you have?
- Do you want granite or a basic countertop?
- Should you replace the windows?
- Should you replace the furniture?
- What type of flooring do you want?

Once you have a scope defined, you can move to the next level of defining the work to be done.

Caution: *You are not looking for a detailed systematic list of tasks here. That detail will hamper you.*

As an example, at this stage, you want a simple objective. Let's examine an everyday task, taking out the trash. You do not want a breakdown of this objective:

- Get off the couch.
- Walk to the garage.
- Grab the trashcans.
- Open the garage door.
- Walk (with cans in hand) to the curb.
- Let go of the cans.

You get the picture. No one manages a task list in that detail. There is just too much detail here for a simple job that everyone understands. Too much detail can be just as confusing as not enough detail.

Let's return to the example of the kitchen renovation project. You could list, to the best of your ability, all the steps, or work to be done, as follows:

- Prepare the kitchen for the project.
- Demolish the old walls.
- Purchase all new fixtures and equipment.

- Construct new kitchen.
- Move back in.
- Close the project.

You might think that this is a good start, but now you want to try to break these areas into detail:

1. Preparation:
   - Empty the kitchen.
   - Arrange for alternative eating and prep area.
   - Store dishes and cookware so they are still accessible.

2. Demolition:
   - Remove the center wall.
   - Remove old flooring.
   - Remove old lighting fixtures.

3. Purchasing:
   - Purchase appliances.
   - Purchase flooring and paint.
   - Purchase light fixtures and accessories.

4. Construction:
   - Frame new wall.
   - Install plumbing.
   - Dry walling and paint preparation.
   - Paint.
   - Install new flooring.
   - Install new appliances.
   - Install trim.

5. Close:

- Arrange for all inspections.

- Move back and arrange dishes and cookware.

- invite family and friends, and have a party!

The benefit in doing this is that it forces you and your team of people or volunteers to think through the project. Soon, you can begin to get a handle on the time it will take and the labor it will take to complete.

 Caution: *By doing this, you might realize the job's true magnitude and be tempted to back out.*

Please don't! That is why we wrote this book—so you would experience the "power of the plan." Every project, big or small, needs a plan. The more planning you do up front, the fewer surprises when you execute the plan and less to fear.

At this point, we want to direct you back to *www.thepoweroftheplan.com*. We hope that you will find one suitable for your use.

Review Points:

Have you written a scope statement listing what is in and what is out of scope?

- What work will be done?

- What objectives will be met?

- What work will not be done?

- What objectives will not be met?

- What does the product look like in detail?

CHAPTER 4

Who Will Do The Work?

We're going to tell you a true story about the importance of selecting the right team and knowing more about them than just their names and skill sets. A company in Scotland had just purchased a competitor from the United States. The merger of the two organizations seemed to go well in the early days, but eventually, it was discovered that the people side of the merger was not going well. Infighting went on between the two old camps, and morale was sinking fast. The friction started at the top. Executives could not agree and approached everything very differently. The effects could be felt throughout all departments. They were in trouble.

The solution to the problem came to them from a consulting company that specialized in human dynamics. Through a personality assessment tool, the company could place personnel in one of four color quadrants: red, green, blue, or yellow. The **reds** were those people who liked to take charge and who were very quick to make decisions. The **greens** were the more considerate team members who wanted everyone to be and feel engaged in the process. The blues were the systematic team members who needed more details and information before ever considering a decision;

and the **yellows** were those cheerleader types on every team who like to bring a little levity to lighten up things. For good or bad, each of these personality types looks at projects and problems from very different perspectives. They even communicate differently!

The newly merged company put their *current* leadership team, drawn from both original companies, through this analysis. They evaluated the results, gathered the senior team into one room, and handed out hats colored according to the personality assessments. As everyone put his or her hat on, the problems became obvious, and the room filled with exclamations of surprise. Some high-profile *decision makers* were not wearing red hats, and some low-profile people were.

It became obvious that the company had misread the skills sets and personalities with which they were dealing. They made some wrong assumptions about their new team. They assumed that the appointed leaders were true leaders. They tried to make leaders out of people ill-suited to lead, and they discovered that they had some real gold on their hands in the junior ranks, which was just misplaced.

This story's moral is simple: know your team. Appreciate that different people bring different skills to the table. Find those skill sets, foster them, and use them well.

Choosing the right people with whom to work is important. If you need people to make a project or initiative succeed, then your ability to source, screen, train, and designate the right people is paramount to your success. You have heard it said that a good manager is someone who surrounds himself or herself with appropriately skilled people.

You might not bring any special skills or training to this project, except your abilities to pick, train, and lead a great team, but these are very valuable skills to have, and they are probably why you were asked to lead the project in the first place. If so, you might already have a group of friends,

family members, or colleagues on whom you can call to help
with this new project.

 An important principle applies in the "real" world
of project management as well, and it is this: the
better you treat the people who work for you, the
more likely they will be to volunteer for your next
project.

If you treated your volunteers or employees badly on
your last project, you will be surprised at how "busy" they
can become when they see you looking for help. David's
father-in-law used to say, "My job is to make heroes out
of everyone around me," which is a great attitude when
treating your workers, whether they are volunteers or
employees. Treat them with respect and consideration.

All right, let's get at it. You must consider some basic
questions when picking your team. They include:

- **Ability**: What skills, talents, and specialized
  training does your potential team member need to
  get his or her job done? Consider whether it is likely
  that you can recruit someone with all the skills that
  you need. You might need to break a job so two or
  more people can share responsibility, or you might
  want to hire someone with specialized skills for a
  short but critical period. For example, if you need
  someone to set up a sophisticated computer program
  to track donations, issue receipts, and generate
  follow-up letters, it might be wiser and more cost
  effective in time to pay someone to do this, rather
  than spending time and energy searching for a
  volunteer.

- **Availability**: Can your potential team member
  finish the project with you? Answering this question
  shows you why you need a clear picture of what each

41

major task will take in time and effort before you start to look for volunteer team members.

 Tip: *Better to overstate the time and effort a job will take a volunteer than to understate it, hoping not to scare him or her off! Be honest with yourself and with your key volunteers. They will appreciate it in the end.*

Here is another consideration when assessing availability concerns. Perhaps your key team members are not available for the project's full duration or are unwilling or unable to commit to the entire project. If so, try to anticipate exactly when and for how long you will need them. You might not need them in the early stages of planning the event, but need their expertise once you have the preliminary plan in place. Or you might need them for a short time only, to put the final changes on the project cost plan. People are more likely to volunteer for a job, even if they are busy already, if you can assure them it will be for only a short period and for a specific task.

- **Experience**: All you need is a team of willing warm bodies for some jobs. Then, there are those jobs in every project that demand someone who has "been to the beach" a few times and has the scars to prove it. We are talking about that highly underrated commodity called experience.

  If you need someone on your team to interface with potential corporate sponsors, for example, you will want someone who is not only comfortable in that role, but has also been in that role or that world and can communicate effectively with those people. Remember, some volunteer team members will be the "faces" of your project to the public. Their role will reflect not only on the project, but also on you. Therefore, choose your key people carefully and look for experienced resources in those roles crucial to your success.

- **Interest and Enthusiasm**: In past projects, we have very often found that people's passion about the project or their role sets them above the rest of the pack. Every project has crucial requirements for people with specific skills, talents, or experience, but they can have all the skills and talents and lack enthusiasm and passion, and then they are a drag on the rest of the team and the project as a whole. We have had to ask some very talented people to step aside, because they showed neither interest nor enthusiasm, to allow someone less technically qualified to do the job.

  A general consideration in choosing your team members is the level of team functionality you need in your project. In other words, how well does the team function together? If you know that there will be times of extreme pressure because of deadlines or logistical complexities, you want and need a team of people who can work well together and function highly. You need to step back and try to see how the team members will work together. Maybe you don't need to assess the entire team's functionality, but the members of your Executive Committee or other decision-making body need to function well together.

Consider that the team is only as strong as its weakest team member is. Ask yourself the following questions about the key members of your team:

- Are they committed to making the team a success? In other words, are they motivated by the prospect of personal glory or prestige, or can they commit to making the entire team a success?

- Are they willing to participate and get their ideas across? Are they committed to do more than simply show up for meetings? Are they reasonably articulate and passionate about their positions without being domineering, or are they prima donnas?

- Are they good listeners? Are they willing to listen to ideas put forth by other team members? Often, the listening skills of team members make a team effective.

- Finally, are they willing to expose and deal with problems? More than any other, this attribute will bode well for a high-functioning team. We have all been in those uncomfortable situations where everyone knows there is a problem, but no one wants to acknowledge it or deal with it.

As a leader, your responsibility is to set the tone and model the behavior that contributes to a high-functioning team. This might mean you have to step out of your comfort zone occasionally, but you are reading this book because we want to help you become the leader you have always dreamed of becoming.

 Tip: Go to the website to see a Personal Skills Checklist you can use with your team members as a team-building exercise and an opportunity to talk to them about team function.

 Caution: *Remember, as team leader, you have two priorities. One is to make sure that the project is successful. The other priority is that you maintain the team throughout the project.*

Often, a successful project is simply defined as finished on time, on budget, and on requirement. In other words, you did what you said you would do. Think of it this way:

if you managed to bring the project in on time, on budget, and on requirement, but you were the only team member left standing at the finish line, and as you look behind you, you see your former team members spread over the battlefield as casualties, have you succeeded? To be a successful leader, you must balance both priorities—task and maintenance. Sometimes, your emphasis will be on getting the task done, but other times, it will be on team functionality or maintenance. A good leader keeps his or her eye on both priorities constantly.

Let's use the fundraising event and the list of work from the previous section as an example of how to set up a team:

- Set the date.
- Book the space.
- Order the food and drinks.
- Get prizes.
- Get speakers.
- Set an agenda for the event.
- Send invitations.
- Manage the money.

Step 1. If any of these sections can be assigned to someone in your "community," then do it. Even though you could do it yourself, we want you to assign it to someone else.

Step 2. Take anything left over that you can do on your own.

- Set the date: you
- Book the space: you

45

- Order the food and drinks: assign

- Get prizes: assign

- Get speakers: assign

- Set an agenda for the event: assign

- Send invitations: assign

- Manage the money: assign

Wow, that was easy! Now, you have a committee of six people working with you. Each has a simple piece of the puzzle to work on. Your job is to communicate, coordinate, control, and help.

Step 3. Ask your committee leads to put together a team around them on the same principle—get others involved. Remember, many hands make for light work.

🍽 Let's go back to the kitchen renovation. We left this project with a detailed list of work to be done. Let's assign that work, remembering that we are on a tight budget:

- Preparation:
    - Empty the kitchen: you
    - Arrange for alternative eating and preparation area: you
    - Store dishes and cookware so they are still accessible: you
- Demolition:
    - Remove the center wall: you
    - Remove cabinets: you
    - Remove old flooring: you
    - Remove old lighting fixtures: you
- Purchasing:

- Purchase appliances: you
- purchase the cabinets: you
- Purchase flooring and paint: you
- Purchase light fixtures and accessories: you
- Construction:
  - Frame new wall: contractor
  - Plumbing: plumber
  - Dry walling and paint preparation: contractor
  - Painting: painter
  - Install new flooring: flooring company
  - install new cabinets: contractor
  - Install new appliances: contractor
  - Trim: contractor
  - Final paint: painter
- Close:
  - Arrange for all inspections: contractor
  - Move back and arrange dishes, cookware, and so on: you
  - Invite family and friends and have a party!: you

 ***Tip**: Distinguish clearly between volunteers and hired help.*

A paid resource requires a clear mandate, scope of work, and contract, despite how trivial the task. Your sixteen-year-old daughter will require a very clear set of instructions, description of work to be done, and, most important, an agreement (verbal is fine here) about how much she will make after completion. Outside paid resources come with their "team," their external resources and tools, and typically require much less "management."

The volunteer is a completely different ball game. Volunteers require much more management, handholding, direction, and coddling. They are great people to work with, but also the most challenging.

 Review Points:

- Have you chosen the right people for the project?

   ° Have they the right abilities?

   ° Will they be available to finish the project with you?

   ° Do you have people with experience where you need them?

   ° Have they interest and enthusiasm?

- Are your key people

   ° Committed to making the team a success?

   ° Willing to participate and get their ideas across?

   ° Good listeners?

   ° Willing to expose and deal with problems?

- Remember to treat your workers with respect and consideration.

- Remember to keep your eye on both getting the task done and on team functionality.

CHAPTER 5

How Much Time will it Take?

U p to now, planning the project has been clear and concise. This next section is not the easiest part of the puzzle. Trying to figure how long something will take to be done can be very difficult, especially when you are not doing the work. As planners, we first need to create an estimate. An estimate is exactly that, nothing hard and fast, just a ballpark idea how long the project will take from beginning to end, which is not as simple to figure out as it might seem.

There are two questions or two parts to this equation:

1. How long will the task take?

2. How much time do you need to get the work done?

It takes only an hour or two to make fifteen phone calls to potential sponsors for your fundraising event, but your volunteer might need two weeks to make those calls.

Whether you are dealing with one person and one piece of work to be done or many resources and many tasks, you must consider that some work cannot start until other work has been completed. A good example of this would be that you can't print the program until you have your sponsors in place, the meal planned, and the order of events decided. These are sometimes called schedule dependencies (one task depending on another to start or finish). Failing to consider these schedule dependencies ahead of time can lead to an unrealistic schedule and disappointed "customers."

The best way to approach this scheduling piece is by, again, thinking through and writing a breakdown of all your project's major work components. We already did this when we defined all the work in the kitchen renovation. You broke all the work down into major components or deliverables: design, demolition, construction, and so forth. Let's use that example to illustrate this idea of schedule dependencies.

You cannot do the construction until you have removed the old counters, cupboards, and floors. So, the construction schedule depends on the demolition schedule. You must know when the demolition will be finished before you can schedule the construction.

 Tip: *Check out the www.thepoweroftheplan.com website to view some plan examples with these dependencies.*

A fact is that, when dealing with any resource, whether volunteer or paid, you must build in what we call "slack," or "float," simply a cushion to allow unexpected delays. You must assume that people will not always meet their deadlines or their estimates, sometimes for good reasons.

If, for example, your printer needs three days to produce your program, you should build in extra time and deliver your final version to them a week before your event. Experience comes into play here. When a resource gives an "estimate to completion," ask yourself, how experienced is this person in doing this work? Can you rely on his estimate? Remember, an estimate is only valid if the estimator is experienced or knowledgeable in that area. Build in your cushion accordingly.

At this stage, you might like to set what are called schedule "milestones," single moments along the planned schedule when you need something important to happen. For example, the points at which you decide to go, or not go, ahead with the campaign, or when you send a final payment to the contractor.

These important flags along the way will tell you that you need to address a problem or need to meet a deadline before anything else happens. These points in your schedule are markers or checkpoints on your map. Schedule milestones do not have durations, that is, there is no time involved.

The first two are obvious, the start date and the end date. You might want to place a few other pins or milestones in your plan. For instance, food must be ordered by this date, a contract must be signed by this date. These milestones keep you and your team on track and alert to the key "deliverables," or components, that are time-sensitive and must be completed either on or ahead of schedule. By developing critical milestones in your schedule, everyone can see the importance of certain tasks. It really is a motivator for your volunteer team.

Let's go back to your fundraising event, look at each step, and break it down into smaller tasks, which will form the basis for your schedule for this project and help you to develop the schedule milestones. Remember, you can't develop a realistic schedule until you know all the work to be done.

- Set the end date—this is the first step in the process, and typically, this has already been done. It is like working backward from the end to the beginning at this stage. You might have to brainstorm with your team to decide a realistic end date or delivery date.

Tip: *Do not delegate this important task to one person. If ever there was a need for "expert judgment," this is it. Get as many people as possible around a table to brainstorm this.*

Tip: *If possible, make sure that your event date does not conflict with other major events in peoples' lives. Events such as NHL playoffs, summer soccer registration night, and Academy Awards night can negatively affect attendance at your event.*

- Start the campaign — After meeting with the committee; determined by the end date

- Manage the money — Every project needs a good comptroller. Good control of revenue and expenses is essential in every project. Get this person in place as soon as possible. Make sure that he or she is available for the duration of the project and can wrap it up at the end.

- Book the space — Once you have the end date finalized and agreed, get this next step done immediately. Spaces to hold events are not sitting around empty waiting for your call. Look around now to see if you can get the right facility at the right time.

- Confirm it — You should have already discussed availability dates with the facility. .

- Send out invitations — This could just as well read, "start advertising." People need to set their calendars. Deal with this one as soon as possible. The more warning people have of the event, the more likely they will be able to fit it into their calendars. Don't underestimate how busy people are. You will need at least one month's notice to give your audience enough time to get it on their calendars. The selling of the tickets might take only a week.

- Get entertainers — Meet with committee to get ideas.

- No later than one month before the event — Develop a program or agenda for the event. Start once entertainers have been confirmed. Remember, the printer needs time to set it up and you need time to get approvals from the committee, if necessary.

- 2 weeks before — Meet with the caterers. Order the food and drinks.

- 2 weeks before — Get prizes; meet with committee to get ideas as soon as possible.

- 1 week before — After meeting with the caterer, confirm decision with the committee.

- 1 week before — Final confirmation of numbers.

- 2 days before — Firm up the catering order and confirm with committee.

Note that we did not detail the work to the level of phone calls, letters, follow-ups, thank-you letters, and so on. As a planner, you need to decide how detailed you want to be in your schedule. In our example, there might be too many of these tasks to detail.

 Tip: Remember to schedule your follow-up meetings or your team conference calls early. Setting these activities into the schedule will avoid surprises and missed meetings later.

One final step in all this, and possibly one of the most important steps, is to hold a "Post Mortem." This is the final meeting when you and your team talk about and document any lessons learned from this project. These "lessons learned" will be valuable inputs into the planning of the next event you or someone else takes on. Now is the time to schedule a date and confirm it with all people on the committee as soon as possible, so they are prepared to attend. Typically, this should be held no later than one week after the event.

As you can see, there is a very logical process to the planning activities, giving you an opportunity to think out all work involved in detail, despite whether it ends up in your official plan. Note that this planning phase usually pulls out red flags or important details you would never have thought of otherwise.

Many of us are inclined to find a way to use technology as much as possible in our lives. This part of the project is a very good example. Someone on your committee, or even in your family, might tell you to use an electronic scheduling tool to do this planning properly. But actually, all you really need is a piece of paper. Better than that, a simple Excel spreadsheet works beautifully. If you are bored and have all the time in the world, and you want to learn to use an electronic scheduling tool, definitely look at the various project management program on the market. But we believe it is overkill for the kind of projects this book addresses.

Going back to our kitchen example, let's look at a list of all the activities and an estimate of the time involved. Again, this will form the basis of the schedule for this project.

	Resource	Duration in Days
1. Preperation		
Empty the kitchen.	You	0.5

Arrange for alternative eating and prep area.	You	0.5
Store dishes and cookware so they are still accessible.	You	0.5
2. Demolition:		
Remove old cabinets	You	0.5
Remove the center wall.	You	1.0
Remove old flooring.	You	1.0
Remove old lighting fixtures.	You	0.5
3. Purchasing:		
Purchase new cabinets	You	1.0
Purchase appliances.	You	0.5
• Dishwasher		
• Stove/oven		
• Refrigerator		
Purchase flooring and paint	You	0.5
• paint		
• flooring		
Purchase light fixtures and accessories	You	0.5
4. Construction		
Frame new wall	Contractor	2.0
Plumbing	Plumber	2.0
Dry Walling and paint prep.	Contractor	3.0
Install new flooring	Flooring Company	2.0
Install new cabinets	Contractor	2.0
Install new appliances	Contractor	1.0
Trim	Contractor	1.0
Final Paint	You	2.0
5. Close		
Arrange for all inspections	Contractor	1.0
Move back and arrange dishes and cookware	You	1.0
Invite family and friends and have a party	You	1.0

Review Points:

- Have you created a project schedule:
    - ° Considering schedule dependencies?
    - ° Breaking down all your project's major work components?
    - ° Building in a cushion for unexpected delays?
    - ° Setting milestones?

CHAPTER 6

How Much will it Cost?

F or many people, creating a budget might be the least enjoyable part of managing any project. However, it is probably one of the most important tasks and should be addressed early in the planning stages of your project. Without properly planning for this aspect of your project, you risk sabotaging the entire project.

Many of us hate the numbers side of all this work, but you need to address this and not put it off. You might be tempted to procrastinate in this area or simply delegate it to someone on your committee, but if you are leading this initiative, it is your reputation at stake. Without meaning to scare you away from taking the lead on this project, just imagine how you would feel if your fundraising event was a huge success in that everyone enjoyed himself or herself, but you lost money on it!

If you delegate responsibility for this to someone else, make sure that he or she is competent and trustworthy. You should spend enough time with the person on this part of the plan that you are well versed in what will happen throughout the project lifecycle.

> The budget is not just costs and expenses; it must also address revenue.

 Here is an example of a very simple budget for a fundraising event.

	Revenue	Expenses
	$10,000	
Advertising		$ 1,000
Room rental		$ 500
Food		$ 2,000
Profit:	$ 6,500	

As you can see, a budget does not have to be complex and difficult to understand. The easy part is putting it into a simple format. The difficult part is collecting all the information and making sure it is accurate and up to date. You need to train your team to keep their records up to date and to pass the information along to whoever is managing the finances for the project so they can record them and provide timely reports to all the stakeholders.

This fundraising project is intended to generate revenue. Let's assume that you are going to sell tickets as the primary source of revenue. How many articles can you sell at what price? Again, it is simple math. The challenge is in estimating the number of tickets you can reasonably expect to sell, which is where experience helps.

If this is your first time running such an event, you need to do some research and digging to find reasonable numbers. This is also where you must practice some risk management. Our advice would be to ask as many people as you can for their estimates. Ideally, you will have some experienced people on your committee or advisory board. If not, make sure that you ask around until you find someone with experience running a similar event. This is called due diligence.

Remember, these are estimates, sometimes called "guesstimates." A good guess that isn't far out of line will help the planning process to move along. The risk management comes into play when you and your committee or volunteer team brainstorm all that could go wrong that would impede or restrict the sales:

- Is there a major competing function planned for the same weekend or even the same month?

- Are the tickets priced reasonably enough so people might buy them, even if they cannot attend the function?

- Have you allowed enough time to get the tickets printed, distributed to the sales team, and to the potential purchasers?

- Have you planned adequate marketing activities to support the sales?

All these, and more, are questions that you and your team need to consider when estimating the revenue that can reasonably be raised.

The same principle of risk management needs to be applied when estimating the expense side of the ledger. Here are some good rules of thumb from someone who has led his fair share of events:

- Pad all supplier estimates by at least 10%.

- Estimate 25% more resources than recommended.

- Include a healthy contingency fund that will cover the unexpected costs.

- Include some money in petty cash for unexpected expenses.

Track your expenses on a regular schedule. If you don't know what is happening on the expense and revenue side, you can find yourself in a lot of trouble in a surprisingly short time. Use a spreadsheet or accounting program or even a simple paper-based ledger that will allow easy updates. Good control over expenses is often missing in work out there, and very often, you can see later that it would have helped make the project successful. Remember, as leader of this project, your reputation could suffer from sloppy or nonexistent financial controls. Keep it simple, but **keep it!**

> **Tip**: *On the risk management side: if you are not comfortable or knowledgeable about bookkeeping, then here is a **big** hint—**get someone else to do it for you!***

Many accountants, bookkeepers, and math wizards out there would love to help. Ask them well ahead of time and get them to show you and the rest of your key team members what they do and how they do it.

 So, back to the kitchen renovation. Let's break out the estimated costs of the project. In a few cases, we might have to break a section out into a little more detail to estimate the costs properly:

1. Preparation:
   - Empty the kitchen: You—$0
   - Arrange for alternative eating and prep. area: You—$0
   - Store dishes and cookware so they are still accessible: You—$0
2. Demolition:
   - Remove the center wall: You—$0
   - Remove old cabinets: You—$0
   - Remove old flooring: You—$0
   - Remove old lighting fixtures: You—$0
3. Purchasing:
   - Purchase new cabinets: You—$3,500
   - Purchase appliances: You
     - Dishwasher: $600
     - Stove/oven: $900
     - Refrigerator: $800
   - Purchase flooring and paint: You
     - Paint: $500
     - Flooring: $1,000
   - Purchase light fixtures and accessories: You
     - All in-estimate: $600
4. Construction:
   - Frame new wall: Contractor—$1,400
   - Plumbing: Plumber—$1,400
   - Dry walling and paint prep: Contractor—$2,100
   - Install cabinets: Contractor—$2,000

- Painting: Painter—$1,400

- Install new flooring: Flooring company—included in cost of material

- Install new appliances: Contractor—$800

- Trim: Contractor —$800

- Final paint: You—$0

5. Close:

- Arrange for all inspections: Contractor—$0 included as part of contract

- Move back and arrange dishes, cookware, and so on: You—$0

- Invite family and friends and have a party!: You—$100.00

You now have three pieces of information in your plan: the work to be done, the person responsible, and the cost. Now is the time to move to a spreadsheet. The information is much easier for everyone to understand once you get the budget in a spreadsheet. One of the key benefits is that it allows you to recalculate estimates as you go. Check out www.thePoweroftheplan.com to see some examples of a spreadsheet.

Once the work begins, you will want to come back to the budget to enter your actual costs, as opposed to your estimates. If you estimated well, they should be close. However, if they are off by a large margin, you will want to know as soon as possible during the project, so you can make some adjustments. An example: the contractor spent double the estimated time doing the preparation because of hidden trouble inside the walls. If you have a well laid-out budget that you can update easily, you can go back, enter the actual number for that section of the work, and then look for upcoming expenses you might be able to cut back.

In the end, you might still come in within budget, although maybe with downgraded appliances.

Here is what this plan might look like on a spreadsheet:

	Resource	Duration in Days	Cost
1. Preperation			
Empty the kitchen	You	0.5	$0
Arrange for alternative eating and prep area	You	0.5	$0
Store dishes and cookware so they are still accessible	You	0.5	$0
2. Demolition:			
Remove old cabinets	You	0.5	$0
Remove the center wall	You	1.0	$0
Remove old flooring	You	1.0	$0
Remove old lighting fixtures	You	0.5	$0
3. Purchasing:			
Purchase cabinets	You	1.0	$3,500
Purchase appliances	You	0.5	
• Dishwasher			$600
• Stove/oven			$900
• Refrigerator			$800
Purchase flooring and paint	You	0.5	
• paint			$500
• flooring			$1000
Purchase light fixtures and accessories	You	0.5	$600
4. Construction			
Frame new wall	Contractor	2.0	$1400

Plumbing	Plumber	2.0	$1400
Dry Walling and paint prep.	Contractor	3.0	$2100
Install new flooring	Flooring Company	2.0	inc
Install new cabinets	Contractor	2.0	$2,000
Install new appliances	Contractor	1.0	$800
Trim	Contractor	1.0	$800
Final Paint	You	2.0	$0
5. Close			
Arrange for all inspections	Contractor	1.0	$0
Move back and arrange dishes and cookware	You	1.0	$0
Invite family and friends and have a party	You	1.0	$100

Review Points:

- Have you created a budget for your project?

    ° Does it address revenue as well as expenses?

    ° Did you pad all supplier estimates?

    ° Did you estimate more resources than recommended?

    ° Did you include a contingency fund to cover unexpected costs?

- Do you have a petty cash fund to cover unexpected expenses?

- Are you using a simple program or paper-based ledger?

- Are you tracking actual figures regularly to control costs?

The Power of The Plan

CHAPTER 7

What are the Risks to Our Plan?

J ulie and Frank's wedding was in the last minute planning stage. Everything looked perfect. And it was. And they lived happily ever after. But it might not have worked out that way—the wedding part, anyway. So many things could have gone wrong as they have with many weddings before theirs:

- The plan was for an outside reception, and it could have rained.

- The dresses might not have been ready on time.

- The best man might not have made his flight the day before.

- The bride might have made a run for it (great movie!).

- The minister might not have shown up.

- And on and on.

Risk is an unpleasant fact for any event, and risk management is a critical step of any project. Although you might think that the risks to your event are minimal, it is surprising what can come out of a brainstorming session with your committee members. The first step in managing risk with any event is to make a list of all the risks associated with your event.

This is an important step, even if you just take an hour to address it. Here is the question: What could go wrong? Your job, and that of your committee, is to brainstorm around anything that could negatively affect your project's outcome. One way to approach this is to ask your team to identify the critical success factors of your project. In other words, what must happen if this event will be a success? You can also turn the question around and ask, "What must not happen if this project will be successful?" Once you understand what the critical success factors are, you can then begin to brainstorm around the identified areas.

There are four questions to ask in this process:

1. What could go wrong?

2. What is the chance it will happen, and what is the impact if it does happen? (Scale this analysis with a simple high, medium, or low rating.)

3. How much control do you have over the risk?

4. What can you do to minimize it?

Try to find some balance here. It can become overwhelming if you get too carried away. You want to exercise due diligence, but not become paranoid in the process. Once you have listed risk events, the next step is to analyze them to determine which risks are worth paying attention to.

The second question helps you make that analysis. You and your team will look at each risk event on your list and try to determine a) what the probability is of that risk occuring and b) if it does occur, the impact it will have. You don't have to be too scientific with this. A simple matrix scaled 1–5 on both the vertical and horizontal axes will give everyone a good idea.

Risk #1 is plotted on the matrix. Let's say it has a low probability of occurring (2 out of 5), and even if it did occur, the impact would be minimal (2 out of 5 again). Therefore, this risk would be considered a low risk. You would work your way through all the risks you identified and try to rate them as high, medium, or low. Let's say that you and your team identified seven risk events, but on analysis, you realized that there were only two high risks (high probability of occurring and high impact) and one medium risk. The others were so low as to hardly register. Now you know which to take the next step on. The low risks are not ones you should lose sleep over, so you can ignore them. Concentrate on the high risks, and keep your eyes on the medium risks. It sounds like a lot of work, but it can identify potential pitfalls in your project.

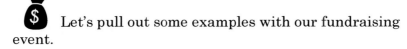

Tip: *Go to the website for examples of this matrix and its use.*

 Let's pull out some examples with our fundraising event.

1. **Weather**. Weather can be a **high risk** depending on your region. We don't need to tell you that you have very little control over Mother Nature, but you can prepare. If the event is outdoors, you could use tents in case of rain. If you live in Hurricane Alley, hold the event indoors.

2. **Entertainers cancel.** Cancellation is a **medium risk.** Again, we might have little control, but we can be prepared with backups. Another idea is to write

in your contract that if entertainers need to cancel, it is their responsibility to supply a backup.

3. **No one attends.** If you are selling tickets for a first-year gala, this is a **high risk**. You have full control if you are sure that your sales and marketing team is well established and working hard.

As you go through the risks that could pop up, you naturally end up with a very good review of all your project details, which is one positive spin-off of this process and with any planning process. The more time you spend as a team looking at the various aspects of your project, the better understanding everyone will have. Good luck!

 And back to our kitchen renovation:

	Resource	Dura-tion in Days	Cost	Risk	Rat-ing
1.Preparation					
Empty the kitchen	you	0.5	$0	none	
Arrange for alternate eating and prep. area	you	.05	$0	none	
Store dishes and cookware so they are still accessible	you	0.5	$0	none	
2. Demolition					
Remove old cabi-nets	you	1.0	$0	none	
Remove the center wall	you	1.0	$0	hidden wires, pipes, etc.	low

Remove old flooring	you	1.0	$0	none	
Remove old lighting fixtures	you	0.5	$0	none	
3. Purchasing					
Purchase cabinets	you	1.0	$3,500	availability of preferred models	med
Purchase appliances	you	0.5		Same as above	med
• Dishwasher			$600	Same as above	med
• Stove/Oven			$900	Same as above	med
• Refrigerator			$800		med
Flooring and Paint	you	0.5			
• Paint			$500	none	
• Flooring			$1000	availability of preferred models	med
Lighing fixtures and accessories	you	0.5	$600	Same as above	med
4. Construction					
Frame new wall	Contractor	2.0	$1400	none	
Plumbing	Plumber	2.0	$1400	Hidden problems lurking from within	med
Dry-wall and paint prep.	Contractor	3.0	$2100	none	
Install new cabinets	Contractor	2.0	$2,000	none	

71

Painting	Painter	2.0	$1400	none	
Install new flooring	Flooring Company	2.0	inc	none	
Install Appliances	Contrac-tor	1.0	$800	none	
Trim	Contrac-tor	1.0	$800	none	
Final paint	you	2.0	$0	none	
5. Close					
Arrange Inspections	Contrac-tor	1.0	$0	Availability of inspec-tor	
Move back and arrange dishes and cookware	you	1.0	$0	May be delayed due to above	low
Invite family and friends	you	1.0	$0	Same as above	low

As you see, there are not many high risks involved here. The contractors or plumbers could disappear or slow and delay everything, but these are only medium risks. It can be difficult to control most risks. However, knowing them and being prepared to deal with them will help you and your committee sleep better.

Remember, though, it is impossible for you and your team to identify all risks successfully. It is also impossible to avoid all risks. The best you can do is to try to identify as many as you can and develop contingency plans to deal with the ones you can't avoid.

Review Points:

- Have you listed all the risks associated with your event?
  - ° What are the critical success factors?
  - ° What must not happen if this project will be successful:
    - — What could go wrong?
    - — What is the chance it will happen, and what would be the impact?
    - — How much control do you have over the risk?
    - — What can you do to minimize it?
- Are you concentrating on the high risks and keeping your eyes on the medium risks?

The Power of The Plan

CHAPTER 8

Follow-up and Control

W ell, here you go; you are on your way! All the planning has been done. Now, it is time to implement or execute those plans. Although it might be true that planning is the most important (and sometimes most difficult) part of every project, you cannot afford to let your guard down now. In truth, this is where many very good leaders drop the ball. They think that all the work is done. The plan looks good, the budget seems realistic, the teams are formed, and all is well. However, at this critical stage of your project, you, as leader, must be extra diligent in making sure that the plan is executed the way it should be.

We could probably write a separate chapter on clever clichés about "plan the work/work the plan"; "follow the map, and you won't get lost"; and so on. The thing about clichés, though, is that there is usually some truth to them. It is not only frustrating for your team to have a leader who fails to follow the plan, but it is also disastrous for your project.

Particularly at the beginning of a project, you want to be in control. The easiest way to do that is to follow the plan. There is much to be said about starting well. In every project, whether big or small, the more quickly you can develop momentum the better the project will run.

Think about the huge kickoff events you have attended for United Way or the Cancer Foundation. The organizers of these events realize the importance of developing momentum early, which is why it is so crucial to have your first few days or first few activities well planned and well staffed so they go off without a hitch. This then becomes the crucial phase of the project. You must stay on top of everything.

This is not to say that there will never, or can never, be glitches. If it is obvious early that the plan is flawed or something happened to change the road map, then only an idiot would continue to follow the plan. This is all covered under the section on risk and change management, so we will talk about it later.

Now is a good time to introduce a few tools or concepts that will help ensure that your project is a success. What we are talking about is the need for you to have, as much as possible, control of everything that goes on daily in your project's life cycle. This is not to say that you need to be thinking, doing, and checking 24/7, like a full-time job; however, it means that you need to know two crucial pieces of information:

1. **Who** is doing the work?

2. **What** are they doing?

The question you must be able to answer at any time is "how are we doing?" or another way of asking, "where are we on the road map? Where are we compared with the plan?" This is not as simple as it sounds because the answer required of you depends on who asks. For example, your banker will want one type of answer; your major stakeholder will want something entirely different.

The bottom line is that you need to know what is happening. And the only way you can know what is happening is through continuous follow-up and control mechanisms built into your plan. A colleague of ours is fond of telling project managers that if they don't know what is happening in their projects, they are a train wreck waiting to happen! This aptly describes how important this step is; hence, the title of this chapter.

So, what do follow-up and control look like? How much is enough and how much is too much? After all, no one, especially a volunteer, likes to be micromanaged. We need to find a balance here. The more experienced of you will know how much follow-up is required. Others, with less experience, will often overdo or under do this step. The reality is that every project needs this, so you need to find a balance and get it done. Timing and approach is the key here. Nagging at your people too often will not win your friends. Leaving them to drown for too long is risky. You must find a balance.

The process here is simple. The difficult part is making it work. Here is the basic process in four easy steps!

1. **Follow up with your key resources regularly.** You want to know how they are doing. How is their work going? What changes to the plan should you know about? To take this step effectively, there are a few things to consider:

    - Who are your **key** resources? In other words, know who will be able to answer your questions and which resources have the information you need at their fingertips.

    - Have you explained to them the information you need and when you need it?

    - Are your expectations of this realistic? Be very clear about what information you want and what level of detail you want, or you might be frustrated with too little or too much information.

2. **Update the plan, making sure that any changes to the schedule or budget are reflected in the new version.** To do this effectively and promptly, you will need some mechanism for tracking changes to the plan and updating it quickly. Remember that we talked about a simple spreadsheet that will allow quick updating. This stage of the project will drive home that tool's value. If you think that your method is weak, look for someone with the requisite skills to build you a spreadsheet or develop a simple tool. Taking time to develop an adequate tool now will save you much time and frustration later.

3. **Communicate the updated plan to everyone.** This step is crucial. Make sure you know who "everyone" is. Do not take for granted that someone will pass on the information to his or her team members. This is one time when you want to over communicate. However, knowing exactly what information to communicate is crucial as well. Not every stakeholder needs to know all the details. As we said earlier, some of your stakeholders will want different information or different levels of detail. All these questions should be part of your communications plan, so you are not guessing at "who needs what and when do they want it" questions.

4. **Do it all again.** We realize that this might sound a little simplistic, but the message we are trying to get across here is that you need to repeat these steps regularly. Once your project begins to roll out, you will need constant updates about how you are doing, actual to plan. Knowledge is power here, and the more information you have the better you and your team will sleep at night. Make this status reporting a priority, and you can relax, knowing that you have control.

Your approach here is very important to everyone involved. Respect everyone's time and schedules. Respect the differences in communication styles within your team.

 Tip: *Check out the website for some examples of status reports and other tools to help you in your follow-up and controlling activities.*

Review Points:

- Do you have control over everything going on daily in your project:
  - ° Do you know who is doing the work?
  - ° Do you know what they are doing?
- Do you know what is happening in your project?
  - ° Do you follow up with your key resources regularly?
  - ° Do you update the plan with any changes?
  - ° Do you communicate the updated plan to everyone?
  - ° Do you repeat the previous three steps regularly?
- What about milestones:
  - ° Did you list all the milestones?
  - ° Are they realistic?
  - ° Are you tracking them?

CHAPTER 9

Manage Change

Yes, things change. Change is inevitable, so a wise leader will anticipate it and plan to manage the changes. We all can think of projects or events where an unforeseen change caused all kinds of trouble for the team and others. Although it is difficult to anticipate what precise changes might occur, it is not difficult to develop a plan that will allow the orderly management of all changes with a minimum of panic or finger-pointing.

Having a change management plan in place will greatly ease the tension associated with unforeseen changes, and it will contribute to quick turnaround on important decisions that must be made about changes to the original plan. Managing change, reacting to change appropriately, can often make or break not just our projects but our teams as well. A wise leader plans for the inevitable changes that occur in all projects.

We have all seen it—a team lead or key team member quits; a general contractor disappears; a crucial delivery of materials is delayed; the list can go on and on. A change management plan should allow you, as team leader, to keep any resultant delays to a minimum, keep all the stakeholders calm, and bring together the key team members who can make a remedial decision quickly and

81

efficiently. A good change management plan should allow an analysis of risks associated with proposed options. It should not involve the entire team, but only the senior members of the team and any members who can contribute to an analysis of the proposed options.

An effective change management plan also considers how your team members will communicate any changes that occur. Although we will deal with this in detail when we discuss communications, let it be said here that the communication of changes is crucial to your success. For now, we will assume that you will have a reporting system for status updates on the project. The important principle here is to make it easy and comfortable for your people to report any changes.

Let's face it, most often a change is bad news. Have you ever worked for someone who doesn't want to hear bad news, or are you one of those leaders? This is what we mean by making it difficult for team members to report a change. If there is a climate of fear on the team, or you make it too complicated for people to track and report changes to the plan, you might never hear about them. Although this might sound like a good solution, what you don't know in this regard can and will hurt you!

We know that this might sound a little daunting, but it is not. As always, the key to successful projects is planning. We are simply planning for our response to any changes that come up during project execution. So, let's take it one step at a time.

Step 1. Take a deep breath!

Most important, **do not panic** if an unexpected change occurs, try to see the big picture. We plan to avoid panic. A good change management plan will automatically trigger some immediate responses and actions.

The first thing you need to do in this step is to understand the significance of the change. For example, if the change is the resignation of a minor player on the setup team for the fundraising dinner, it is not a big deal, and the impact is minimal. However, if it is the resignation of important player such as the financial comptroller, the significance is much greater and the impact is major.

You should get all the facts straight before you respond. Is the information accurate, and can you verify it? Once you understand exactly what the issue or change is, it is much easier to formulate a response. The second part of this first step is to notify the appropriate people on your team. If there are financial implications, you should include the treasurer or comptroller. If it is a facility-related change or issue, the chair of that subcommittee would need to know, and so on.

Step 2. Go back to the plan.

You should stick to the plan at this stage. Too many projects fall apart because the team begins to panic and forget the road map they are supposed to follow. As leader, you want to ensure that the team sticks to the plan until it is deemed appropriate to abandon it.

Ask yourself, does this change affect any parts of the plan, either negatively or positively? Look closely at all the details.

 Principle: When you take a hit in one element of your project plan, there will always be a ripple effect in other parts of the plan.

If the printer just announced that there will be a week's delay in getting the tickets printed, where will the ripple effect be? It could be the overall event schedule; it might affect the HR aspect of the team; it might affect the budget.

All these elements are potential sore spots because of a delay in one area. You might want to adjust the schedule. Immediately contact any resources whom this will affect. Look at the budget for potential impact.

Step 3. Communicate with all the appropriate stakeholders.

We will talk more about this in the next section, but this is a crucial part of step three. Think about who needs to know what because of this change. Again, remember the ripple effect principle. It would be advisable to err on the side of communicating with too many people rather than taking the chance of forgetting someone. A helpful tool might be an issue log or change log. You can view examples of these tools at our website. The important thing is to communicate clearly why the change is being made and what the impact on the overall plan will be. The sooner this communication goes out, the better.

Step 4. Monitor the change.

Is the alternative action you put in place working? Will it be necessary to make further changes to the plan? How is the team responding to the changes?

This is also a good time to do a small post mortem on how well the change management plan worked. Were you able to analyze the situation accurately? Were the right people notified and brought together promptly? Were the change and agreed response communicated to all the stakeholders? Were you able to assess the results of the change accurately? The answers to these questions will determine whether you need to do more work on your change management plan.

The next change or issue is probably already in the works!

 Review Points:

- Do you have a change management plan in place?
- If a change occurs:
    ° Take a deep breath and assess the significance of the change.

    ° Go back to the plan.

    ° Communicate with all the appropriate stakeholders.

    ° Monitor progress closely for a few days as you move forward with the changes to the original plan.

The Power of The Plan

CHAPTER 10

Communicate, Communicate, and Then Communicate Some More!

It might surprise some of you (unless you are a veteran of projects) that the leading cause of project failure worldwide is lack of communication. That is based on projects managed by full-time project managers! No wonder this is often considered the most difficult part of any project—communicating effectively.

The easiest way to approach the communication plan is to ask yourself these questions:

- **Who** needs **what**?
- **When** do they need it?
- **How** do they want it?

Let's deal with the who first. With whom do we have to communicate? In the world of project management, we call these people stakeholders. These are all the people who have a stake in the project. They are either interested in or affected by your project.

The stakeholder's impact can be either positive or negative.

In other words, if your project will result in someone else's project being delayed or canceled, that person would still be considered a stakeholder. As you think about this, it can seem a little overwhelming. However, not everyone who you have identified needs to be constantly updated on every aspect of the project. Some will be communicated with simply through an announcement or newspaper article. Others can be very important to the success of the project.

How to tell the difference? Ask yourself this question: **who can make or break my project through its life cycle?** In other words, try to narrow it to identifying exactly who is mission critical to your success. You want to communicate with these people often and effectively. Here are some examples of mission critical stakeholders:

- Your teams of workers, both volunteers and staff
- Your suppliers
- Your owners, sponsors, or customers
- Your family

On the **what** side of things, you are asking yourself two things: (1) **what** makes this person or group a stakeholder, and therefore, (2) **what** information do they need? This is called stakeholder analysis. Is it important? You bet it is! The better you and your team understand the stakeholders' needs, the better you can manage their expectations around your project.

We know that this sounds like over-the-top project management, but most projects fail because not enough time and effort were put into this step. Ask yourself, "What do they **need** to know?" Of course, not everyone needs, or wants, the same information. By doing this analysis, you will avoid over communicating with some and under communicating with others. Like all planning work, time spent here will save you time later. You might approach it as follows.

Your workers need a regular flow of information around the work to be done, with deadlines and budgets. They might need this weekly early in the project and daily closer to launch day. Your suppliers need to know what you need and when and how it should be delivered.

Again, timing is important here and can vary. The owners, sponsors, or customers need to know how the project is progressing, or the project's status. They need to know that everything is moving along smoothly—and they need to know when it is not. It might not always be good news. But the sooner you can warn people of disasters, delays, or disappearances, the better off everyone will be.

Your communication plan should be designed to give you all the status information you need promptly so you can communicate it to others promptly.

> *Your family needs to know what you are doing, especially if it involves any commitments during personal times: evening meetings, early-morning conference calls, travel away from home, and so on.*

When? When do they need the information? As noted above, the timing on project status information can vary depending on what stage or phase of the project you are in. Although monthly meetings might be sufficient very early in the planning phase, weekly and even daily meetings or updates might be needed as you draw closer to launch day.

The stakeholder with whom you are communicating influences the timing. Your team should probably hear from you weekly depending on the work they are doing. Your suppliers really don't want to hear from you at all unless there is a change in plans. In this case, you might ask permission to touch base once or twice to be sure the materials are "in the works." The owners, sponsors, or customers might want updates once a week, but again, it depends on what their role is and at what stage of the project you are.

Many of us have heard people say, "I wish I had known this earlier," or "please give me regular updates," and even, "don't bug me!" It is very difficult to predict this part of the puzzle, so the only way to know is to **ask**. Ask each of these groups how often they want to hear from you, or better yet, suggest to them a schedule of communication. Some might not know the answer, so a suggested schedule would help them.

Tip: *It is wise to think this through with your team and set some boundaries around how much information you will convey and how often you will be distributing it. Otherwise, you might find that some stakeholder is constantly asking you or team members for another update on the status of the project.*

We can't give you a golden rule here for timing, but the important message is that you need a schedule for regular reports to all these people. Set up a schedule, communicate it to everyone, get an agreement, and do it.

Now, let's deal with the **HOW**. How do they want to get the information? What format is best?

Our first recommendation is always **keep it simple**. Keep the information as brief and concise as you can. If anyone wants more information, let him or her ask. It is better to under deliver in this case than otherwise. People do not want long, drawn-out drivel about the minutiae of the project. If you provide too much information with too much detail, people will not read it. Therefore, you are **not** communicating effectively! Think about what they **need** to know and deliver just that—no more. Everyone loves to receive information delivered quickly, efficiently, and clearly. They will be very impressed and grateful if you can do this.

On the delivery method, or format, we have many options that will help get the information out. In this information age, we have more options than we can probably use. Some will be more effective than others and the team members should decide what works best for them. Here are some suggestions and a brief discussion of the pros and cons of the most common methods:

- meetings
- phone calls
- e-mail
- letters
- texting or instant messaging

Meetings

Meetings can, and should be, one of the most effective means of communicating with all your stakeholders. Unfortunately, they often are a killer. Not many people like them because, honestly, very few meetings are well managed. If you are going to call a meeting, you must be organized and efficient about it. Below are some key ingredients for a great meeting:

Here are Some Roles you May Consider

- **A chairperson**, typically the project lead. The chair keeps it moving, keeps everyone engaged, and prevents one person from dominating the discussion. The chair allows everyone to have a voice, if required.

- **A timekeeper**. We are firm believers in sharing the pain and sharing the glory. Ask someone to play this role for you.

- **A scribe.** Someone to take minutes, preferably a neat writer or fast typist.

Purpose

Have a clear objective and communicate it clearly to everyone. Why are we here? What are we trying to accomplish?

Agenda

The agenda should not be too tight, not so full of items to cover that it will be impossible to do it all. Stick to the stated objective. If it is not on the agenda, it isn't discussed. Include time for introductions, if required, and time for a recap, if required.

Timeline

A timeline should have a firm start time and firm stop time clearly communicated. No one likes meetings that go beyond the advertised stop time (it is disrespectful to all present as well), and no one likes to arrive on time to see the meeting delayed as you wait for stragglers. If they are going to be late, that's their problem.

 Caution: *If you wait for stragglers the first time, and they get away with it, they will be perpetually late!*

Follow-up Items to Consider

- Distribute meeting notes or minutes to everyone afterward, including action items.

- Action items must include an assignment to someone and a due date.

Some Final Thoughts on meetings

Your meetings should **not** include one-on-one discussions or reviews that do not concern everyone. Keep these to another time and another method. If everyone needs to hear from all parts of the puzzle, set a time limit for each update. Coach everyone on keeping it simple and brief. If you need to hear updates from various committees, have the committee lead prepare a written report and distribute it to the attendees before the meeting. Then, receive it as a report and ask for questions, for clarification only, during the meeting.

Your meeting location is also important. Meetings should be held at convenient locations for everyone, not just the lead. The location should be conducive to the number of people involved and the required space.

If you are meeting before 10:00 a.m., provide coffee; over lunch hour, make the food situation clear to everyone (bring your own; you will provide; we are going to a restaurant; you will pay; each person will pay).

Phone Calls

The phone is easy, convenient, and fast. If there is more than one person, consider using a conference call facility. Conference calls are inexpensive and accessible to everyone, typically through your local phone provider. Without seeing faces, you sometimes lose the power of a meeting, but your attendance rate will be better and everyone will appreciate not having to travel to every meeting. Use conference calls for updates, crisis management, and any meeting that can be handled well without seeing faces. Conference calls can also include those team members outside a reasonable commute.

Here are some things to consider if you are using a conference call:

- As much as a strong facilitator makes for a great face-to-face meeting, it is even more important when you are leading a conference call.

- Have an agenda, preferably sent to everyone by e-mail before the call. Do not try to accomplish too much in a conference call. Have only one or two objectives at most.

- Keep focused and keep track of the time. Honestly, if your conference call goes much beyond thirty minutes, you are probably kidding yourself if you think people are still focused.

- Use some kind of protocol to keep everyone engaged. For example, insist on only one person speaking at a time; have people identify themselves **every** time they speak, unless only two or three people are on the phone.

- Set time limits per topic area.

- Send out as much background information as possible ahead of time so people can be prepared to discuss the key issues.

- Always end your meetings with a recap and action items.

- Make sure that you send out the minutes as soon as possible.

E-mail

Much can be said for the benefits of electronic media for communicating; however, very few people know how to make these media effective. Please allow us to remind you of some e-mail basics in the interest of effective communication.

It can easily be misunderstood! Science has discovered that only 7% of what we communicate to others is made of the words we speak. An additional 38% of what we project to others is made of vocal qualities such as tonality, volume, timbre, emphasis, and speed of talking. And 55% of what we communicate is entirely nonoral nonverbal and consists of body language (posture, facial expressions, gestures, and so on). So, while communicating by e-mail is very easy, quick, and efficient, it is typically not done very well. Given the information above, is it any wonder misunderstandings and issues arise when we rely too heavily on e-mail? After all, our audience is only getting about 7% of the message.

- E-mail is a great medium for communicating facts and figures, or data related to sales of tickets, and so on. It is perfect for communicating the minutes of your recent telephone conference call or even your face-to-face meetings. Reminders, notifications, and quick notes of encouragement or appreciation are all handled well by e-mail. But please think carefully before trying to bring people to some agreement or decide on various alternatives by e-mail. Then, it becomes far too slow, time consuming and burdensome for it to be effective.

- CC (stands for carbon copy, for those readers who don't know what a typewriter is) only those who need to read it, not the world, please.

- As with meetings and phone calls, keep it brief and to the point. E-mail messages should not replace a good old document prepared by your word processor. If you have much to say, put it in a Word document and attach it to a brief e-mail.

- If you might ever need proof that someone received your e-mail, use the feature that will return a message to you once delivered, but never leave this feature on all the time. This is rude.

- Only use the urgent sign (which often comes out as a red exclamation mark) when you really mean that it is urgent. Urgent means that you need a response immediately and that the communication is time sensitive.

Letters

It sounds old-fashioned, but we still use letters, mailed through the good old postal system. Try it someday. If you want a powerful medium to thank and motivate members of your team, try a handwritten note on good stationery. Again, old-fashioned — perhaps. Powerful — watch what happens! It will make a very good impression.

Texting or Instant Messaging

Don't. Full stop! There is no record of the communication, and the medium is much too personal. Leave texting to you and the kids and your friends.

We started this section by saying that lack of communication is the leading cause of project failure worldwide. We want to remind you again that successful project managers make communication a priority. It is crucial to your success to take the time to identify all the players (stakeholders), understand their needs and the difference in their needs and expectations from others, and develop a communications strategy to keep everyone happy. Your team will appreciate it, your suppliers will appreciate it, and your customers/sponsors/end users will appreciate it. Good luck!

Review Points:

- Do you have a communication plan:
  - ° Who needs what?
    - Who are your stakeholders?
    - Does your family know what you are doing?
  - ° When do they need it?
    - Have you set boundaries around how much information and how often?
  - ° How do they want it?
    - Meetings?
    - Phone calls?
    - E-mail?
    - Letters?

The Power of The Plan

CHAPTER 11

Close the Door

W ell, folks, here we are! It seems like a long time
ago that we talked about "Opening the Door" and
walking through. Now, it is time to think and plan
about how we will close the door at the end of the project.
Many of our projects often end with a bang, literally—
with fireworks, or applause, or those great words, "Ladies
and gentlemen, thanks to you all, we have raised $10,000
tonight for our wonderful cause." At work, it might end with
a simple e-mail that says, "Congratulations, it launched."
Later, it might end with a glass of wine and a major sigh of
relief.

But before any of this happens, you need to ask yourself,
"Is it really finished?" Usually, it isn't finished because of all
that must be done to wrap up. This next section addresses
that issue and offers some helpful tips to make sure you can
enjoy that glass of wine.

Finish Well

We have talked to literally thousands of professional project
managers from all kinds of projects and most of them have
one thing in common. If you asked them what stage or
phase of any project is hardest to manage, most will tell you
it is the final phase, or the close, of a project.

Many volunteer leaders and project managers share the same sentiment. It just seems so difficult to finish well. It is difficult to keep your team focused when they can sense the end is near. It is human nature to begin to relax a bit as the project winds down. After all, the event is over, the consensus was favorable, and everyone on the team is tired, right? Your job is to hold their feet to the fire a little longer to make sure that all the details are completed. This is what makes this step so difficult. Finishing well is as important as starting well and executing well, but it is so often ignored or minimized.

The good news is that with some planning, this stage can be done quickly and efficiently and leave everyone feeling great about what was accomplished. The secret is in planning for what needs to be done to close the project.

This might include immediate needs, such as a teardown crew or vehicles to transport borrowed or rented furniture, stages, sound equipment, and so on. It might also include financial considerations, such as collecting all the money from ticket sales, paying all the suppliers and vendors, and developing a final financial status report for the stakeholders. Think ahead about thank-you letters, news releases, reports, and other communication needs. Can any of this be done before the actual close?

In the next two sections, we will talk about the last steps—the handoff and the celebration—but, for now, try to think of any loose ends that must be planned by and organized with your team.

 Tip: *If you have many willing volunteers, such as a youth group, service club, or even a local scout troop, consider using a new team to do some closeout work.*

Your front-end team might well be on the verge of exhaustion and would welcome some fresh talent and muscles to do some cleanup work. The same might be true for the financial side of things. Now would be a great time to bring in that volunteer accountant who said she would love to help but had limited time to offer.

In short, if you are going to finish well, this phase of your project must be planned just as carefully as the other stages. No one likes to have a project hanging over his or her head long after it was supposed to finish. Wrapping it up completely and promptly will ensure that you have willing volunteers the next time you take on a project.

Handoff

This step might or might not be relevant to your project, but we wanted to include this section because, like finishing well, the handoff is often fumbled, and the project isn't completely successful. A handoff might simply be presenting a big check to the charity for which you were leading the fundraiser, complete with press releases and other media involvement. Or you might want to step down as leader of a successful team and let someone else take over. Your project deliverables might even be a small part of a bigger project, such as an advertising campaign or marketing campaign. Whatever the situation, some key elements will make this step easier and more effective.

The first of these elements is communication. No one likes to step into a new role or take over from someone when there is little or no information about the project, the team, the status to date, or the financial details. Keeping good records and archives of correspondence can be very helpful to someone coming in.

Probably one of the key elements that will make the handoff successful is called simply "lessons learned." Make sure you follow through with your plan for a final team meeting or event that will allow you to hear from everyone about the key lessons he or she learned from this project. It is asking, "What went well?" "What can we improve on?" and "How would we do it the next time around?" Make sure that you document these suggestions and include them in the archives for the next team.

 This will be the first planning input for the next team and will avoid many repeated mistakes.

Celebrate

Everyone likes a party, and you and your team probably deserve one. What can we say, except this is a smart and effective way to make sure you have a willing team next time? The secret ... you guessed it—**planning!**

You and your team will probably be too exhausted or too relieved that it's over to start planning after the event, so do it now. Use the KISS approach here: **K**eep **I**t **S**imple! It doesn't have to be extravagant or glitzy, just sincere. It can happen immediately after your project launch, or it can be later when the dust settles, but make sure that everyone knows the date and details well ahead of time.

Make the celebration significant without making too much work for yourself. People might be willing to pay something toward it, but it must be appealing to them. Again, consider jobbing this step out to a third-party volunteer team. It takes some fresh enthusiasm and creativity to make this a success. Finally, make sure that those who cannot attend are recognized at the event and sent a thank-you card.

This is an important part of any project and goes a long way in establishing real team mindset with your group of volunteers. Have fun!

Review Points:

- Have you planned what needs to be done to close the project?
- If relevant to your project, have you planned for handoff:
  - ° Will there be good records and archives of correspondence?
  - ° Will there be a final team meeting to collect "lessons learned"?
- Have you planned a celebration?

Conclusion

Congratulations on your decision to open that all-important door! Good luck with your project. May you complete it with a smile on your face and with friends, family, and colleagues saying thank you. Our hope is that all those people who help you achieve your goal will be excitedly waiting for another opportunity to work with you. You are now on your way to becoming that effective leader you dreamed of being.

About the Authors

DOUGLAS LAND is an award winning Trainer, Coach and Consultant in the areas of Project Management; Communications; Contract Management and Organizational Effectiveness. His background includes training and consulting work with many private corporations in the U.S.A. and Canada; municipal, regional and provincial governments as well as many Aboriginal groups and organizations. He has extensive experience in Construction projects; Community Development projects; Business Development projects; Power Generation Plant Turnaround projects; Oil and Gas Industry; Real Estate Development.

He is the President and Founder of Lobstick Project Solutions Inc.; a training, coaching and consulting practice. He is also Program Director, Western Canada, of the Masters Certificate in Project Management, Schulich School of Business, York University and a member of the faculty. Doug is also Senior VP, Atocrates Project Sciences International.

DAVID BARRETT is the founder and now Managing Director of ProjectWorld, ProjectSummit and BusinessAnalystWorld. He is the Program Director of the Masters Certificate in Project Management and The Masters Certificate in Business Analysis offered through the Schulich Executive Education Centre, Schulich School of Business and in partnership with nine other universities across Canada. He is the founder of ProjectTimes.com and BusinessAnalystTimes.com. He recently launched the new Canadian Leadership Summit on strategic and strategy execution. David is also a keynote and dinner speaker on various BA and PM topics and he has two books coming out in early 2013.

He is also the Director of PMPeople.com, a web site connecting project managers with Charities and Not-for-Profit organizations.

Did you like this book?

If you enjoyed this book, you will find more interesting books at

www.MMPubs.com

Please take the time to let us know how you liked this book. Even short reviews of 2-3 sentences can be helpful and may be used in our marketing materials. If you take the time to post a review for this book on Amazon.com, let us know when the review is posted and you will receive a free audiobook or ebook from our catalog. Simply email the link to the review once it is live on Amazon.com, with your name, and your mailing address—send the email to orders@mmpubs.com with the subject line "Book Review Posted on Amazon."

If you have questions about this book, our customer loyalty program, or our review rewards program, please contact us at info@mmpubs.com.

Are People Finding Your Meetings Unproductive and Flat?

Turn ordinary discussions into focused, energetic sessions that produce positive results. If you are a meeting leader or a participant who is looking for ways to get more out of every meeting you lead or attend, then this book is for you. Ida Shessel's *Meeting With Success: Tips and Techniques for Great Meetings* is filled with practical tips and techniques to help you improve your meetings. You'll learn to spot the common problems and complaints that spell meeting disaster, how people who are game players can effect your meeting, fool-proof methods to motivate and inspire, and templates that show you how to achieve results. Learn to cope with annoying meeting situations, including problematic participants, and run focused, productive meetings.

Available in print and electronic formats from most local bookseller, Amazon.com or directly from the publisher at **www.mmpubs.com.**

Are Your Projects Stonewalled by Negativity and Pessimism?

There is an old saying that "your attitude determines your altitude." People with a positive, constructive attitude achieve much greater success than those with neutral or negative attitudes. *Today Is A Good Day! Attitudes for Achieving Project Success* by Alfonso Bucero explores the impacts of attitude on project success. Examining the importance of a project manager's attitude in motivating a team, dealing with project stakeholders, and overcoming issues, the book contrasts the outcomes of both positive and negative attitudes. Full of case studies illustrating the key concepts, the book shows how project managers can change their way of thinking, plan for success, take advantage of the power of commitment, convert project issues into opportunities, communicate more effectively, deal effectively with negativity and fear, and effectively use persistence to increase the chances for project success.

With the right positive attitude, problems seem to melt away. Don't get caught up in negativity surrounding project issues and risks, because... Today is a Good Day!

Available in print and electronic formats from most local bookseller, Amazon.com or directly from the publisher at **www.mmpubs.com.**

Become a Better Negotiator!

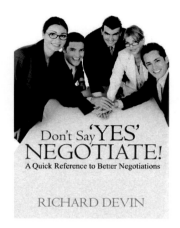

We all do it, every day. We do it before we even get out of bed in the morning. The alarm clock clicks on—the insidious buzz of the alarm chips away at your slumber—and what do you do? Smack the snooze button. You have just begun your day... negotiating!

This is an easy-to-read, easy-to-understand, practical book for negotiating in the new millennium. This book is filled with strategies and techniques that you can implement immediately. The book contains unique and often humorous contemporary approaches to negotiating compiled from real life, real world scenarios. It will quickly enable you to identify the key factors in any negotiation by: thinking before you speak; maintaining emotions; asking for something you want, and then asking again; asking for something you don't want; saying no; not turning a buyer into a shopper; discovering aspiration levels; deciding what is reasonable and what is ridiculous;discovering the three tenses of any negotiation; determining ethical flexibility; being greedy, stingy, and selfish; and more.

Don't Say Yes – Negotiate! by Richard Devin is the perfect "on the go" guide that will enable you to quickly identify the other side's tactics and strategies and allow you to defend yourself ensuring better negotiations for both sides. It makes absolutely no difference if you **negotiate at garage sales, at home, or at a major corporation—you can become a better negotiator.**

Available in print and electronic formats from most local bookseller, Amazon.com or directly from the publisher at **www.mmpubs.com.**

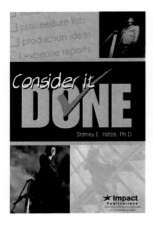

Having Trouble Finishing What You Start?

Do you begin worthwhile projects only to let them fall by the wayside? Psychologist and life coach, Dr. Stanley Hibbs, outlines ten simple prescriptions to help you plan, organize and complete any worthwhile project. Topics include goal-setting, overcoming excuses, persistence, and battling the fear of failure. *Consider It Done! Ten Perscriptions for Finishing What You Started* is an ideal book for those wanting to start a new business venture but who are struggling to get started.

Available in print and electronic formats from most local bookseller, Amazon.com or directly from the publisher at **www.mmpubs.com.**

THINKING ON PURPOSE
FOR PROJECT MANAGERS:
OUTSMARTING EVOLUTION

BILL RICHARDSON

Learn to Overcome Automatic Reactions.

When you're facing down a lion on the open savannah, automatic reactions hardwired into your system through eons of evolution can save your life. However, when you're trying to impress the CEO across a boardroom table, those same responses can cost you big time.

So, how do you overcome your automatic reactions, retrain your brain, and outsmart evolution? By learning and using the techniques revealed in *Thinking on Purpose for Project Managers: Outsmarting Evolution* by Bill Richardson

This book will teach you:

- How evolution has hardwired your brain to think on autopilot, using mindsets you don't know about to make decisions you don't control.

- How thinking on autopilot affects your performance results and ultimately your professional impact.

- How to identify and navigate around the "mindfields" of biases, emotions, and habits that cause these problems.

- The five-step Thinking On Purpose process that can help you take control of your thinking by learning when to "reset" versus "repeat".

- A set of tools that can help you structure your thinking for better clarity and creativity.

- How to transform your team by helping them learn to think on purpose and create the mindset that there is no problem or adversity they cannot solve.

Available in print and electronic formats from most local bookseller, Amazon.com or directly from the publisher at **www.mmpubs.com.**

The Power of The Plan